# IN THE MEANTIME

LaRhonda N. Felton

In The Meantime

LaRhonda N. Felton

Copyright © 2018 by LaRhonda N. Felton.

All rights reserved.

No part of this original work may be reproduced in any way without permission from the author, except by a reviewer. For interviews or any inquiries pertaining to the content of this publication, please contact the author and/or publisher.

Email: LaRhondaNFelton@gmail.com

Facebook.com/AuthorLaRhondaNFelton

Instagram: @Author_LaRhondaNFelton

Edited, Formatted, and Published via *iWrite4orU*
www.iWrite4orU.com

Cover Image Obtained from iStockPhoto.com:
Photo ID 187272584

ISBN: 978-0-9998842-2-5

Library of Congress Control Number: 2018908551

Printed in the United States of America

In The Meantime

LaRhonda N. Felton

## Dedication

This book is dedicated to three individuals: Melissa Felton Henderson; Etrec J. White and Janaver Wooden. You all have pushed me in your own way to do something with my writing. I appreciate each one of you. You each have taken time to read and provide me with very honest feedback.

Melissa, sissy, you've read almost everything I've written. You always let me know exactly what you think with a sincere and gentle approach.

Etrec, you facilitated the introduction to Liltera and I couldn't thank you more.

Janaver, my sister, you've also read so much of my writing. You always keep it sincere and with love.

The three of you aren't afraid to call me and let me know when I need to get it together. Thank you all for being in my corner, being firm when I needed it and being a very big part of this project's completion. You have no idea how much your support and friendship mean to me. I love you all and thanks again.

In The Meantime

LaRhonda N. Felton

**Table of Contents**

Shattered............................................................9
Addiction...........................................................15
Phone Sex..........................................................17
Invisible............................................................19
Midnight Creeper...............................................21
Sex Scene Pt I....................................................23
The Heart of The Matter.....................................27
23......................................................................29
Dilemma............................................................31
Sapiosexual.......................................................33
FWB..................................................................35
When Darkness Arrived.....................................37
Jewel Pt I...........................................................41
Late to Work......................................................45
Thanks, Baby.....................................................49
Nobody's Leaving..............................................51
No Sleep............................................................53
Stressful Day.....................................................55
Anticipation.......................................................57
Intoxicating.......................................................59
Paranoia............................................................61
Jewel Pt II.........................................................63
Exposed............................................................65
Reciprocity.......................................................71
Love.................................................................73
The Trench.......................................................75
What He Does to Me.........................................79
Soul Snatcher....................................................81
Watching Him..................................................83
Forgiven...........................................................85
Him..................................................................87
Champagne......................................................89
In the Moment..................................................91

In The Meantime

Gin & Cologne..................................................93
Longing............................................................95
Falling in Lies..................................................97
Karma...............................................................99
She is Me........................................................101
Pass or Fail....................................................103
Assets.............................................................107
Gone................................................................109
Blackout.........................................................111
Secrets............................................................113
Confession.....................................................115
Broken............................................................117
Acknowledgments.........................................121
About the Author...........................................123

LaRhonda N. Felton

## **Shattered**

So, we had a fight
And he left
I'm so pissed
Couldn't control myself
It's been so much pressure
Trying to maintain
And he's so nonchalant
Like I can't feel his pain

The pain was unbearable
We both lost that night
Our baby boy born way too early
He had no chance to fight

Ever since then
He's had this look
Like I made a choice
And my soul was shook
No words were said
Just tears and sobs

My heart shattered
My entire life robbed

The ride home was worse
I couldn't stop crying
He couldn't look at me
Just driving and sighing
What the hell could I do?
I had all these plans
That just fell through
The hourglass, grains of sand
We can put away the blue paint

## In The Meantime

And cancel the crib
I don't want to feel
This way ever again

Months have passed
And he still barely talks
I just keep leaving the house
Taking these long walks
Something happened today

That made us both snap
I could no longer take
His silent treatment crap

I asked him if
He felt it was my fault
He just looked at me
Like he hated me
And I was lost
After all, this pregnancy was a shock
Nothing we planned
We wanted to raise our son together
Him showing him how to be a man

Life has a way
Of always throwing a curve
But for him to think I did this
He had some nerve
So, I let his ass have it
Yelling, crying, and cussing
From the minute we left the hospital
And suddenly, I'm nothing?

Oh, I don't have feelings
My son was inside ME

LaRhonda N. Felton

How dare you feel you have the lead
On how bad we're hurting
What could I have done
To cause myself this pain
To go on with life
Knowing I may never smile again

And to think I just knew
He would be there
We would get through this together
The pain we felt, we'd share

It's not my loss or his loss
The loss is ours
Do you even know how often
I cry in the shower?
I tried to shield you from my pain
Because I knew you were hurting too
I never ever thought of
Accusing you
I can't do this anymore
It's over and done
It hurts too much to look at you
Because you look just like our son

I look in your eyes
All I see is him
Your ears, your nose
Your lips and even your chin
My heart breaks daily
Every time you walk in
'Cause I look at you
And it happens all over again

So maybe I need a break

## In The Meantime

A chance to truly recover
Right now, he's not even my friend
And we're so far from being lovers

He stormed out
Slamming the door
I went to bed
I couldn't take anymore

The next morning, he comes back
I hear him inserting his key
He's on my side of the bed
He says, "Baby look at me"
I can't
It causes too much pain
Looking at his face
Seeing my baby again

"Look at me baby"
He turns me over
He kisses my lips
I notice he looks older
This pain has had us both
In our own personal hell
We just ignored each other
Attitudes like, *oh well*

He gazed into my eyes
Which immediately filled with tears
I see my baby boy
When I look back into his

He lifts my face
And says, "Baby we will get through

LaRhonda N. Felton

It will take a while, but I'm here
I can't lose you too

I never ever blamed you
For the loss of our son
If anyone loved him like me,
You were the only one
I just didn't understand
How you could keep praying
I was so mad at God
I didn't know what you were saying
After all this time
We get our first son
And He takes him away?
The very first one?
I didn't know how to handle that
I'm still angry and confused
But being without you
That's way more than I can stand to lose
I love you baby
I need you in my life
Say that I can stay
Say you'll be my wife…"

For the first time in a long time
I looked at him and didn't cry
It was like seeing him again
For the very first time
This was the man I loved
Long before we met

God had shown him to me in my dreams
Ingrained him in my heart so I wouldn't forget

In The Meantime

"From the very first day
I always knew
That I would spend the rest of my life
Loving you
Prayer is all I know
That's how we'll make it through
God answers prayers
How do you think I got you?"

LaRhonda N. Felton

## **Addiction**

Just to smell his cologne
I crave to be close
To be held in his arms
I need a dose

I start to feel sick
As if I can't go on
Whenever he isn't around
It's been too long
My body won't function
Without his pheromones
It's like a constant withdrawal
Whenever he's not home

How do I get over it?
How do I shake this shit?
He has no idea
How bad the cravings get
My mouth begins to water
My movements become slow
I start to feel faint
Until he walks through the door

I don't want to talk
I just need a dose

A sniff of him wearing
Ralph Lauren up my nose
Some days I spray the room
And walk around naked
I need him bad
Hell, I can't take it
Maybe I need rehab

In The Meantime

>  Or possibly an intervention
> Speak openly on this affliction
>      I dare not mention
>
>      I need my fix daily
>    I won't survive without it
>     He has me so turned out
>     There's no doubt about it

LaRhonda N. Felton

## Phone Sex

Suddenly
The texting became too much
My vibrating cellphone
Made such a fuss
Phone to my ear
Him on the other end
Almost in a whisper he says
"Get her wet again"

I hear the lust in his voice
It causes me to shudder
I touch her as he instructs
My legs turn to rubber

He has me so turned on
He has no idea
I want him inside me
His breath in my ear
Controlling my body
Responding to his commands
Cumming on his tongue
I'm putty in his hands

He's showing me something different
This is all new to me

Learning new ways to explore
Through phone calls and sexting
With my Bluetooth in my ear
I listen to what he says next
I never knew I could be this turned on
Through erotic conversations and phone sex

In The Meantime

LaRhonda N. Felton

## **Invisible**

It's funny when he says
"I can't read your mind"
Yet when it's about sex
He's always right on time
Disrespectful as hell
Always got hoes in his face
Then I'm overreacting
When I need space

I stop and take a pause
Before I kill this nigga
Playing with my emotions
My finger always on the trigga
He ain't all that
Not worth my freedom
The dick got me hooked
All his lying and cheating

I got to find a way out
Leave his ass alone
He's clouding my head
My thoughts are no longer my own
His mouth says he loves me
His actions say otherwise
I'm amazed I'm still here
Witnessing my own demise

I'm not myself
Not who I used to be
Smiling and happy
Footloose and carefree

In The Meantime

I got this albatross
And I've been down for the ride
What was alive is dead
And I'm hella tired

I must give up the ghost
No matter the cost
Free myself
Walk away with dignity
Before I have none left
I've given him so much
I no longer recognize myself

Learn from my mistakes
He can have this stuff
Leaving all I own behind
This lesson is heavy enough

LaRhonda N. Felton

## **Midnight Creeper**

He's in bed
Been asleep for a while
But this gin in my system
Got me feeling wild
His back is to me
As I slide into bed
I scoot close behind him
And reach between his legs

Semi-hard
I stroke him slow
He's turning over
'Cause he already know
He says, "Hey baby
Where you been?"
I say, "Out with the girls
I drank too much gin."

I slide in closer
My tongue in his mouth
I don't stop stroking him
I need to cum and now
He touches my lips below
Zoning in on my clit
I was already gushy
Now his fingers are slick

Coming home to daddy
To fan this flame
He dicks me down
Until I scream his name
He knows I'm about to cum
He's kissing me deeper

In The Meantime

>He says the gin always
Turns me into his midnight creeper

LaRhonda N. Felton

## **Sex Scene Part I**

The flashbacks are crazy
It's never felt this way
All the things we did
We didn't see one single sunray

He came into town
And let me know where he was staying
He said, "Bring a bag and don't be late
Bring your ass to me and I'm not playing"

I blush and smile
Swallowing the apprehension
It's been a long while
But he will alleviate this tension

I arrive at the hotel
277 is the number to his room
I knock on the door
Nervous energy causes me to swoon

He opens the door
Kisses me and takes my bag
He leads me to the tub
Candles are lit
He's created a sexy scene

He kisses my neck
And then undresses me
He's staring at me
Taking everything in
If his eyes were fire
There would be a burn on my skin

## In The Meantime

We bathe each other
And it's slow and deliberate
He pours my favorite wine
He's so considerate
Once on the bed
We waste no time
Our position of choice
None other than 69

Licking and sucking
We can't get enough
He slaps my ass hard
But not too rough
I cum so hard
My legs are shaking
He keeps on going
Saying, "Baby you can take it"

He turns me over
Ready for penetration

His dick slides in slow
*Oh my*, the sensation

Long, slow strokes
He's feeding it to me
I close my eyes
Because my vision is blurry
Every fiber in my being
Is set ablaze
He sucks on my tongue
Waking me from this sex induced haze

How far this goes
You have no clue

LaRhonda N. Felton

Keep an eye out
For the Sex Scene Part II

In The Meantime

LaRhonda N. Felton

## The Heart of The Matter

I must remind her
Not to fall too fast
Slow down just a bit
The feeling may pass
If I could control her
I would rule the world
Erasing the pain
Between boy and girl

He has her captivated
And oh so intrigued
She just needs to slow down
And listen to me
I'm the rational one
I think before I leap
But he's seducing her
Even as she sleeps

She claims she's being cautious
Thinking everything through
I know that's the case
To herself she must be true
So, this guy has her smitten
I pray she doesn't fall apart
But what do I know? I'm just her brain
Trying to protect her heart

# In The Meantime

LaRhonda N. Felton

## **23**

We argued about the break up
The reasons he cheated and lied
We yelled and screamed
He never knew how much I cried

It was my birthday
He came with a gift
He could've kept that shit

By the time we finished yelling
He turned to go
Heading for the door
I said, "Don't go"
He turned and came back
Kissing my face
Telling me he loved me
Asking if his errors could be erased

I was lost in his arms
Loving how we were together
We always seemed to fit
Like a stamp to a letter

Our passion deepened
Before we could stop

We were in my bed
And I was on top
Making love like we used to
Sexy and so sweet
He kissed me everywhere
Even the bottom of my feet

In The Meantime

        For an hour or two
    We captured what we'd lost
    We soon came back to reality
    And escaped our brain fog

          It was over
    And that was certain
    This love affair ended
      I closed the curtain

LaRhonda N. Felton

## **Dilemma**

Oh, my dilemma, where do I start?
To let him know the feelings of my heart
Can I be that open, honest and true?
To say *hey, I'm really feeling you*
To see where it goes, where it may lead
To finally know the answer, if he's feeling me

To start something new, see what's next
Have actual conversations and not just text
Or do I leave it alone and wait for his move?
Keep quiet, let him show and prove

I'm afraid of the outcome
A good friendship coming undone
Everyone around me says let it be known
This is new to me, being the vulnerable one

I don't want to be rejected
My heart, I must protect it
But for love to come in, I must be open
Leaving room for anything, even my heart being broken

Lord, I look to you to guide me and see me through
Help me make a choice that you approve
I said I would tell him and see where it leads
Going in with my heart, bare on my sleeve

# In The Meantime

LaRhonda N. Felton

## **Sapiosexual**

He has my full attention
From day one my mind was gone
He makes love to my mind all the time
Therefore, he keeps my mind blown

Scintillating conversations
Fun and serious, yet always deep
I'm a true sapiosexual
And deep down a real freak

He's masterful with his words
Keeping me so intrigued
Never a dull moment
He always aims to please

Conversing beyond the stratosphere
Taking my mind on high after high
His shit is like outer limits
Lost in the stars, I won't even lie

He has his shit together
He's smart and well poised
Different than all that came before him
He's a man, and they were boys

Compare him to others
There's no competition
He's got me so turned on
The others just hoping and wishing

To be in his shoes
There isn't a chance in hell

## In The Meantime

He makes love to my mind
Keeping me under his spell

I don't yearn for more
The conversations are pure and focused
I've fallen in love with him
Being mind fucked and I'm hopeless

I must admit
I'm very impressed
That's not easily done
So, I digress

The man blew my mind
Right from the start
Once my mind was seduced
Only a matter of time before he would have my heart

LaRhonda N. Felton

## **FWB**

He wants to lock me down
Make me his exclusive
Relationships are choking
Cutting off my airway like a noose

I must be free
Like a lioness to roam
Calling him only
When I want to bone

He's good in that way
Breaks me off proper
Trying to cake up, I'm not
Get my back broke and I'll holla

The next time I feel horny
Or the next time I feel the need
To let his presence be felt
Between my knees

He thinks he has all the sense
Shit, I like fun
So why is it a problem
When I use him to make me cum?

Get out yo feelins
This is real life shit
How can I take you seriously?
When did you turn legit?

Hell, I'm just keeping it real
That's what you wanted, right?

In The Meantime

Now you sulking and mad
When I don't spend the night

You made this arrangement
Friends with benefits
Now you switching up
Because you can't handle it?

C'mon dude, I thought we were good
Keeping it on the low
Now you are introducing me to friends
Opening and closing car doors

It's funny how shit changes
You filling my car with gas
All of this began when you
Thought all you wanted was some ass

LaRhonda N. Felton

## **When Darkness Arrived**

Suddenly there's a darkness in my eyes
That beautiful amber glow is gone
There's a coldness in my presence
No longer is it warm

You know you're the reason
Behind the obvious change
I don't say much anymore
Rarely even calling your name

You begin to wonder if you can fix it
The hole you dug in my heart
You have no idea how deep it is
Or where you can even start

It all began with a few late nights
Then, lies about where you'd been
I believed what you said
No doubts and no questions

Then you're suddenly always on your phone
Quiet tones and hushed conversations
I took you at your word
Not pressing for explanations

The day my world caved in
I decided to go out for a change
In a quiet corner of the restaurant
I hear laughter, and someone call your name

I look up like any normal person would
What did I expect to see?

In The Meantime

Surely not you standing there
"Baby, I'm just working," is your excuse to me

You look right into my eyes
And suddenly drop your head
The beginning of the end
Not much left to be said

The woman you're with
Notices the exchange
Her laughter is gone
She's calling your name

I leave money on the table
Quickly racing outside
I can't do this in public
I hold it all inside

My heart shattered that day
Into a billion tiny pieces

I loved you with everything in me
You sneaking and lying for whatever reason

I had to know the answer
That wasn't up for debate
I got home and took a seat
Prepared myself to wait

No matter how long you took
I wouldn't move from that seat
You would have to explain
Why you'd been lying to me

LaRhonda N. Felton

You arrived a minute later
And as if right on cue
You're staring at me
Looking lost and confused

I don't say a word
This is your shit show
You will need to say something
And I will let you go

In The Meantime

LaRhonda N. Felton

## **Jewel Pt I**

Well, suspicion got the best of me
And I picked up his phone
He was in the shower
He didn't even know I was home

Text messages from his brother
Friends and coworkers, maybe this is lame
Before I could put it back, the vibration makes me jump
And there is an unfamiliar name

No picture comes up
That's odd and quite rare
He loves pictures
Why isn't there one of her there?

If I open the message
He will know that I snooped
If I don't open it
This will all be of no use

The shower is still going
So, I touch the screen
The phone comes back to life
The light casting a bright beam

Her message seems very intimate
Asking him how was his night
He told me he was exhausted
Having to take the redeye flight

What did she mean
Am I reading too much into this?

In The Meantime

The shower stops suddenly
Is there something I've missed?

Who could she be?
She's in his phone as Jewel
I delete the message
I must play this cool

He comes into the bedroom
Towel around his waist
"Hey baby," I say
A surprised smile appears on his face

He didn't expect me home so soon
I got off early, is that a crime?
I've thought of him all week
I was looking forward to some alone time

"Hey baby," he says
As he gathers me in his arms

Kissing my lips and neck
I have cause for alarm

I ask him how was his flight
He says long and tiring, but that he missed me
After most trips, he's always horny
Today it stops at kissing

Am I in the twilight zone?
We've been apart all week
And he ends our embrace
With a lousy kiss on the cheek?

LaRhonda N. Felton

He's hiding something
What could it be?
I need to know who Jewel is
And just what the hell is happening

In The Meantime

LaRhonda N. Felton

## **Late to Work**

He's pulling and tugging
Trying to get me out my clothes
He already knows
How this story goes

We both have to work
And shouldn't be late
He's so impatient
He doesn't want to wait
A few measly hours
Until we're home again
He wants me now
And I'm trying not to give in

But with his naked chest
Pressing against my bra clad breasts
He's hard
And I can feel it
Stabbing my thigh
I look at the clock
It's 6:55

I must be
To work by 8
But with all this pressure
He's gonna make me late

He makes me weak
So, he grabs my ass
And down we tumble
In a tangled mass

## In The Meantime

My panties are soaked
As he suckles my throat
He rips my panties
The pretty black lace
I give him a look
*Those you will replace*

He looks at me wildly
And I feel him slide inside
We both breathe deep
And begin to glide

Breathing hard
He doesn't stop
As my first orgasm
Begins to rock

He sighs and moans
I continue to moan
As I clench and
Tighten around him

He smiles and pushes deeper
I can barely keep breathing

It feels so good
He can be so hood
His breathing is erratic
It won't be long
Before he cums
He's twitching and shaking
It's almost done

It's hot
It's quick

LaRhonda N. Felton

Oh, I love this shit
He looks at me
And laughs
We both need a bath
If we go together
We won't make it
To work
Ever

## In The Meantime

LaRhonda N. Felton

## **Thanks, Baby**

My baby comes in and I know right away
That this wasn't a very good day
He doesn't say a word, no need to
I know exactly what he needs me to do

I walk up and kiss his face
Up and down his back, my fingers trace
I take off his shirt as he kicks off his shoes
Our lips never part, while his body gives me clues
That he's missed me all day
And his tension is melting away

Our kissing is so strong and hot
That neither one of us is going to stop
I straddle his lap, massaging his shoulders
Kissing his abs before I move lower

His breathing is sharp and he's biting his lips
He pulls me down hard for a deep kiss
This is what he needs and I'm happy to oblige
I look deep into his eyes as I prepare to ride
To take away all the stress of his long day
And let out his aggression in the best way

This is what I do for the man I love
He's been sent to me from God above

We sweat, we moan in the best love fight
He will sleep very well tonight
He won't think about the stress of his day
My loving him takes all of that away

In The Meantime

As I hold him in my arms and he nuzzles my neck
This lovemaking we won't soon forget
As he grips me tighter and is fully satiated
I hear him whisper groggily,
"Thanks, baby, I really appreciate it."

LaRhonda N. Felton

## **Nobody's Leaving**

The four walls are closing in
He's no longer my lover, not even a friend
It's as if true love walked away
Slowly but surely day after day

Talks became fights
Long days and even longer nights

Who is this stranger that I once loved?
No more picnics, kisses or hugs
It's weird how it happened, almost like a blur
I don't know how to fix it or if I even care

I used to think we shouldn't give up the fight
At that time, it all felt right
Then again, maybe we should call it off
And leave this mess
End the hard feelings, cut out the stress
I don't like him and he hates me
This can't continue, feels like an eternity

My heart aches at the love we lost
He wouldn't man up and I grew tired of being the boss
I can do bad by myself, that's what they say
This has been pure hell far too many days
Maybe I loved his potential, what I thought I saw
I'm so damn angry and hurt, my emotions are raw

He's like a ghost that won't go away
Haunting me endlessly in every single way
I don't like this and it makes me sad
But this distance between us has gotten very bad

In The Meantime

He's sleeping around, he thinks I don't know
Hell, why should I leave?
He needs to go
We're both stubborn as hell and that's the hitch
Now he wants to talk, ain't this a bitch?

LaRhonda N. Felton

## **No Sleep**

Can't go to sleep, he's on my mind
Body so tight, I can't unwind
Needing him close, my hands in his dreads
Loving his scent all over my bed

Kissing his face, his lips and his neck
Rubbing his throat, his shoulders and pecs
His body is hard in all the right places
I touch his spot and watch him make faces
He can't touch me yet, it's against the rules
So, I can have my way with him and watch him drool

Coconut is my massage oil of choice
The mere touch of his skin makes me instantly moist
He doesn't even have to penetrate
Just tasting his tongue makes me quake
I suck his tongue gently, savoring each minute
He's ready to slide in deep and I can already feel it

The aggression in his kiss
He's making a fist
He's on overload
So ready to explode
I set him free
Now he can touch me

He goes straight to my center
Positions himself and prepares to enter
My breath is in my throat
Gasping from every stroke
I start to feel flushed
I can't take much more
He makes me wait, to even the score

In The Meantime

I beg and plead
He gives in to me
There's the release like a broken dam
I truly enjoy making love with this man

LaRhonda N. Felton

**<u>Stressful Day</u>**

When I come into the house
He's sitting on the couch
Everything is nice and neat
I give him a look
I hope he's cooked
Because quite frankly, I'm beat

He takes my purse
And hangs my coat
Before I can ask, he clears his throat

He removes my shoes
And begins to rub
My neck and shoulders as I head to the tub
Rose petals and candles are all I see
Bath oils and a glass of wine he's placed here for me

It's not an anniversary or my birthday
Just another day of the week
He takes a hairpin and pins my hair back
Whispering to me, "Baby relax"
He undresses me slowly and kisses my lips
My neck, my forehead and my nose on the tip

My love for him is unwavering
The tub jets my body's savoring
Before placing his hands in the water,
He rolls up his sleeves
It's a beautiful thing to know
He's been thinking of me
He knows when I'm stressed
He has my moods down pat
He looks at me and says, "I'll be right back."

In The Meantime

He returns with a bowl
Of strawberries and black grapes
Only to find me half awake

He's stroking my thigh gently
And whispering to me, "Baby wake up"
Looking into my eyes very intensely
He says, "I need you to know
How far I will go
To show you what you mean to me
The day you said *yes*
And gave me a chance
To be your lover and your husband
That day made me the happiest man
You really changed my life
When you said I do, and became my wife"

As tears fill my eyes
I try not to cry
I've been blessed with such a great guy
He always knows exactly what to say
To completely erase
Any trace of a stressful day

LaRhonda N. Felton

## **Anticipation**

He ignites passions so deep
Ones I haven't felt in a while
I have butterflies and goosebumps
Like Christmas morning when I was a child

The desire is so strong
Pulling me like a magnet
Some days I'm so weak
I can barely stand it
The things I want to do to him
I want to burn into his memory
Causing smiles and a love he adores
Every time he thinks of me

My body responds to his voice
Like no other before
It's strange but familiar
He keeps me wanting more
My mind is intrigued
My sensuality set on high
No one has ever had me this captivated
That's no lie

He has yet to touch my body
But somehow it seems he has

Maybe those times in my dreams
Or maybe another life in my past
Either way, I can't wait
For our sexual exchange
For him to bring me Ecstasy
And his first taste of Champagne

In The Meantime

LaRhonda N. Felton

## **Intoxicating**

Those in love games: *you hang up… no you hang up*
If only the initial giddiness remained
Butterflies in your stomach
Being in love and being insane

Wanting every waking moment
Spent staring in his eyes
And every night that falls
Him between your thighs

Constantly on a cloud with no parachute
Being in love can be very intense
You have no reason to come down
You lose all common sense

In The Meantime

LaRhonda N. Felton

### **Paranoia**

So, it finally happened
Sex after six years
Feelings are mixed
Happy, sad, full of fear

Did I do the right thing?
Did I make the right choice?
Did I give up my power?
Did I lose my voice?

Feeling conflicted
And confused
Did I miss any signs?
Was I being used?

Will he no longer check in?
Is he suddenly unavailable?
Did he just hit and quit?
Am I incapable?

Is my judgment off?
Am I losing my flavor?
Did he mean the things he said?
Or was it all just playful?

What do I do now?
I can't take it back
Things I said, I meant
There's no way to retract

In The Meantime

> I guess I keep on this journey
> See where I end up
> Hopefully in love in the end
> And not just fucked

LaRhonda N. Felton

## **Jewel Pt. II**

He asked if I would make him a sandwich
That he wanted to go to sleep
I said, "Sure baby, I'll hang in the living room"
He says, "No, I want you right next to me"
So, when I return to the bedroom
He's already under the cover
I stop and stare at him
Realizing how much I love him

I put his sandwich beside him
And go to take a shower
He says, "Thanks baby"
As I bend to pick up his towel

Who the hell is Jewel?
I've got to figure this out
I can't jump to conclusions
But I feel some doubt

My shower is hot
Just what my body needs
I could use a good sex session
To give me even more relief
So, I come back in the room
He's nowhere to be found

Candles are lit
Purple roses all around
He comes up from behind
His arms around my waist
What is all of this?
Surprised look on my face
Suddenly there's music

## In The Meantime

And he covers my eyes
He says, "Baby come with me
I have big surprise"

He leads me to our living room
And sits me in the chair
He removes his hands
I see more roses in there
He gets down on one knee
And takes my hand
He says, "You checked my phone
Almost ruined my plans

Jewel is the decoy
I used to throw you off"
He pulls out a diamond
I choke, so I begin to cough

He laughs and asks
"Baby you alright?
The reason I took the redeye
I had to have this ring for tonight
You've been here with me
Through ups and downs

I love you and I need you
My life is incomplete when you're not around

So, say you'll stay forever
And always share my life
Baby, will you marry me?
Will you be my wife?"

LaRhonda N. Felton

## **Exposed**

The flowers have arrived
The ceremony can begin
I see all the faces
Of our family and friends

This is a special occasion
One we won't ever forget
Everyone is in attendance
Every single guest
I made the list

I made all the plans
I didn't leave one detail
In anyone else's hands

This had to be perfect
There was no other way
They would all bear witness
To the look on your face
See this isn't any happy day
It's a day of exposure
I pray I push through
Maintain my composure

The hurt and betrayal
All of your lies

Have come back to bite you
I've planned your demise
The trickery and fuckery
Will soon be over
No leprechauns or magic potions
No unicorns or four-leaf clovers

In The Meantime

Just your secrets exposed
For all the world to see
You made your biggest mistake
When you decided to play me

Give him just enough rope
He will soon hang himself
You won't pull this bullshit
On anyone else

Come into the party
And take your assigned seat
Soon you will know why
I was so anxious to meet

Your wife is front and center
I met her a while ago, we were both shopping for you
How was I supposed to know?

She asked for my opinion
On the color of a tie
She said her husband had a big meeting
He needed to look fly
I laughed and smiled
Thinking of you
Saying to myself
My fiancé has a big meeting too

I was picking out cologne
We both wanted you to look nice
Us buying for the same man
I didn't even think twice

LaRhonda N. Felton

Purple and black
The tie I loved best
She agreed and before she could leave
I smiled and suggested a vest

She thought the idea was great
Made her selection and turned to leave
I overheard the sales clerk call her name
I got weak in the knees

I waited until she left
To question the sales girl
Married for six years
Her knowledge of you rocked my world
That's when this plan came to mind
That she needed to know
This 3-carat ring on my finger
Wouldn't soften the blow
Then you showed up to my house
Wearing the tie and the vest
I was quiet for hours
Hoping you would soon confess

Even told you of my encounter
With the woman in the store
You kept on talking about making love to me
My story was such a bore

So, this plan had to be complete
With a party full of family and friends
Your lying ass would be exposed
All of it coming to an end

In The Meantime

So, as I walk to the podium
Your eyes as big as saucers
You suddenly look around the room
Into the eyes of your sons and daughter

I start with the day we met
How you chased me down
Wanting to take me out
Since I was new in town
Dinners and movies
Concerts and plays
Weekends at the lake
I was in a daze
You spent crazy money
Nothing was ever too much
I am still so in love
With my Hermes clutch

This lie has caught you
And it's ruined a lot of lives
Were you planning to have a harem?
A city full of wives?

You're looking so dumb
Is that supposed to be remorse?
We must pick up the pieces
And move on of course

Your wife is sobbing
And your mother can't move
What were you really doing?
What were you trying to prove?

LaRhonda N. Felton

Your boys in the back
Are waiting to see what's next
Co-workers just staring
Almost everyone is perplexed
Not me, though
This is exactly what I proposed
Separating the truth from the lies
Leaving you naked and exposed

# In The Meantime

LaRhonda N. Felton

## **Reciprocity**

As the clock strikes twelve
He still isn't home
I have no idea where he is
He hasn't even called
But let me stay out late
He is putting out an APB
Calling and texting
Sweating the hell out of me
That old saying goes
What's good for the goose
He's getting a real dose
I'm finna get loose
Sip me some drinks
Pop my fingers
Leave the phone in the truck
And pretend I'm single

As I head to the truck
Phone rings and it's too late
He should pray I'm home
Before day breaks
I might stop for breakfast
Really do it up
He gone be mad as hell
And so the fuck what
He done pissed me off
It's gonna be the last time
I'm showing all the way out
I won't change my mind
Phone ringing again
Declined to voicemail
He knows he fucked up
He can go to hell

In The Meantime

> Ringing again
> Declined—*boy bye*
> I ain't picking up
> To hear the lame ass lie
>
> I'm in his purple truck
> Flossin', rims on fleek
> Getting a lot of attention
> Even the jealous ones stop and speak
> But this isn't about them
> He needs to learn this lesson
> Or lose me altogether
> Miss out on his blessing
> I'm the baddest bitch in his life
> Let it be known
> He will regret the night
> He didn't bring his ass home

LaRhonda N. Felton

## **Love**

It's hot, it's cold
It's soft and bold
It's nervous
And insecure
It's weak
But endures
It's short
And long
It's right
And wrong
It's happy
And sad
It's good
And bad
We all want it
We all need it
It's in our grasp
Yet we can't see it
Eyes wide open
And it's right there
In every fiber of our being
Down to the shortest hair
A four-letter word
That evokes so much
Without being spoken
Felt through the slightest touch

# In The Meantime

LaRhonda N. Felton

## **The Trench**

He dreamed I did it
Showed up unannounced
Clad in a trench coat
Knocking on the door at his house

Just me in the coat
Nothing underneath
This is the dream
He described to me

It was a rainy night
He gladly let me in
Questioning deep down
When did this begin

This situation, this thing
That frightens us both
He's dying to know
What's under the coat

He doesn't ask
And I won't say
After all it's me
That's come all this way

If he wants to know
He will need to make a move
He's sitting watching me
Trying to play it cool

In The Meantime

The tension is thick
You can slice it with a knife
He doesn't know it yet
But I'm only here for tonight

He should make his move
And make it quick
I'm nervous as hell
So, I start to fidget

He asks if I want a drink
While heading into the kitchen
Sure, why not
Anything to ease this tension

A sweet red
He brings to me
I sip it
Not too hastily

He's staring at me
His gaze and the coat is making me hot

He kisses my lips
I don't want him to stop

Things begin to move so fast
His hesitation is gone
It's like he somehow knew
I would come here all along

The coat is his fantasy
He didn't think that I would
Turn his dream into reality
It seems that I was misunderstood

LaRhonda N. Felton

He asked if this
Would be something I'd do
*Absolutely* was my reply
*But only for you*

So here I am
Ready for his move
Just me in the coat
What does he do?

# In The Meantime

LaRhonda N. Felton

## **What He Does to Me**

I can't sleep
He's on my mind
Running through my head
I can't unwind
How does he do it?

Taking control
Of my every waking moment
Truth be told
He's my inspiration
I call him my muse
Others desire
To be in his shoes

We've never kissed
But the desire is strong
I can't hold on
It's been much too long
The heat and passion
Longing to become one
My sanity has become undone

I'm not crazy
Well crazy in love maybe
These are just a few things
That he does to me

# In The Meantime

LaRhonda N. Felton

## **Soul Snatcher**

I'm sitting on the bed
As he begins to disrobe
Now, I've seen naked men
Still, my breath is caught in my throat

I try not to stare
And try to play coy
But, truth be told
God has blessed the boy

I know I'm no punk
And I've talked some slick shit
However, I do know my body
This will be a tight fit

He comes toward me
Kissing me slow
His fingers between my legs
Making juices flow
He pushes me back
And grabs my hips
Before I could protest
His tongue was on my clit

I grip the sheets
And scream out loud
He's a cunnilingus master
His instructor would be proud
I squirm and try to move
But he grips me tighter
My vision is blurry
And my head feels lighter

In The Meantime

        I came four times already
        He says it's not enough
        That I shouldn't talk shit
        When I can't back it up

        Who knew it would be this way?
        That this crazy shit would happen
        I guess I've finally met my match
        I call him my soul snatcher

LaRhonda N. Felton

## **Watching Him**

His Issey Miyake teases my nostrils
He's a tall drink of water and I want a glass full
I watch him daily
As he comes and goes
He walks with confidence
Strong and bold

His clothes are always immaculate
Tailor-made to fit
His beard trimmed to perfection
Not out of place a bit

I wonder if he knows I'm watching
He turns around, coming my way
Right in front of me he's stopping
"Excuse me," he pauses quickly to say
In a chocolate baritone
Did someone turn up the heat?
Suddenly, I'm so warm
"Yes," I ask, "You need some help?"
"Can you tell me where the conference room is?"

*I know where my room is*
I think to myself
"Yes, I can show you," I reply politely
"I'd love the escort," he says ever so slightly
I come around the desk
To lead the way
I turn to see if he's following
Instead he's watching me sway
"Right this way"
I break his trance
He's looking me up and down

## In The Meantime

His eyes doing a dance
"Are you new here?" I ask
Pretending not to know
He says, "Not so much
But, I've seen you before"
"Oh yeah?" I ask
Acting quite surprised
I turn to look at him
He's staring me right in my eyes
"Yes," he says "a pretty lady
Never escapes my view
I've been hoping to get the chance
To get to know you"

"Really?" I ask
Not sure what I should say
Can't let on
I've also been watching him every single day
"Would it be presumptuous of me
To ask for your number?"
"Not at all," I reply
For his phone he begins to fumble
Another whiff of that cologne
It's making me weak
I need him to hurry
So I can get back to my seat

He saves my info
Says he will call me later
I walk away knowing
My day couldn't have started any greater

LaRhonda N. Felton

## **Forgiven**

This last argument was the worst
We screamed, we shouted, and cursed
And even in that moment I knew
I didn't want to live without you
In our moment of disagreement
I missed our happiness and contentment
I wanted you to grab me and say
"Baby I love you, it will be OK"

We're in separate rooms
I hear you sighing
I feel your gloom
The TV is on and I'm not watching
Tears are falling with no sign of stopping

I get up to wash my face
We meet in the hall, such a small space
You pause for me and I pause for you
Our eyes say everything
We know what to do
At the same time, as if in a song
We both admit what we did wrong
I forgive you and you forgive me
We realize being together is the best thing
You hold me close and I'll never forget
Our first and last worst argument

In The Meantime

LaRhonda N. Felton

## **Him**

He's my favorite R&B song
He's my right when everything seems wrong
He's a hand in the small of my back
He's pushing me to achieve things that I lack
He's my rainbow at the end of a storm
He's my comfy blanket that keeps me warm
He's my comic relief when I need a laugh
He's a major piece of my epitaph
He's my source of light when all is dark
He's the man that holds the key to my heart
He's my dividend on my highest investment
He's what I prayed for, God's blessing
He's the wind that blows on a hot, sunny day
He's my GPS when I can't find my way
He's what I know is right in this world
He's my man and I am his girl

# In The Meantime

LaRhonda N. Felton

## **Champagne**

She's fluffy and soft
And oh so inviting
Just the type of place
You'd want to spend the night in
She purrs and grips
She makes you say her name
She can be wild and sweet
She will drive you insane

She's not easy to get
But so worth the wait
Once you're inside
Oh, the smile on your face

She's wet and soft
She makes you moan
You want to stay forever
With her, you feel at home

If you touch her just right
She gets even wetter
You try holding back
Trying to keep it together
She grips a little more
Getting just a bit tighter

You think you can last
Trying to pull an all-nighter
She swells a bit more
Pulling you deeper
You can't let go
Because you need her

In The Meantime

> She pulls you in
> And holds you tight
> You close your eyes
> And give up the fight
> You thrust some more
> And now you can't move
> She holds you in
> Controlling the groove

I've lived with her forever
I've even given her a name
She's so sweet and smooth
I call her champagne

LaRhonda N. Felton

## **In the Moment**

I can feel me kissing his lips
I can feel him gripping my hips
I can feel me loving his grip
Standing on my toes, him not letting me slip

I can feel him come in close
Wanting more, he needs a dose
Feeling his body crave
A need only my love can save

He's been with other girls
But my love is his drug
He gets high and can't come down
He can't breathe if I'm not around

Intoxicating and invigorating
I am his choice
He's at attention from the sound of my voice

I was made for him
He was made for me
Together, we are synergy
Greater together than apart
The fire was there from the start
An eternal flame that's bright and hot
Love won't quit, love won't stop

In The Meantime

LaRhonda N. Felton

## **Gin & Cologne**

We're at a party laughing and drinking
I catch his eye, he knows what I'm thinking
Every time I looked up he was watching me
Licking his lips and his eye kept winking

I brushed up against him on purpose
Merely passing by
As I bend over in the cooler
I know I've caught his eye

He makes his way over to me
Leaning towards my ear, whispering and kissing
I let him know I'm ready to leave
Ready for bed, but I'm not sleepy

We thank the hosts for the great invite
Let them know we're calling it a night
He places his hand on the small of my back
Waiting on the valet to bring the car
We make small talk and gaze at the stars

The wind blows and I get a whiff of his cologne
Hurrying to the car, I can't wait until we're home
He gets in the driver seat and strokes my bare thigh
I reach over and kiss him, deeply staring in his eyes

He puts the pedal to the metal
We're both a bit buzzed
Hurrying home so we can make love
Between the gin and his cologne,
I'm completely in a zone

In The Meantime

He pulls into the garage and that's as far as we get
His hand between my legs and I'm soaking wet
I unzip his pants, his manhood jerks
Between my hands and mouth, he goes berserk
He reclines the seat
I go to work

The gin and his cologne
I'm too far past gone
We're stuck in the garage
Hell, at least we made it home

LaRhonda N. Felton

## **Longing**

Feelings of euphoria
Always on a high
Waiting to hear his voice
Seeing his smile
My heart stops
When my phone rings
He says, "Hey baby"
My heart sings

Endless hours of conversation
Playing the hang-up game until we both lose
Late nights become early mornings
Finding myself waking up phone still next to me
A text 'good morning'
Indicates he's thinking of me

If he could see my face
He would know he's made the right move
Love is on the horizon
I don't know when, I don't know where
Somehow, we both
Ended up right there
We can't get enough of each other
We lock out the world when we're together
Dinners and movies
Walking the beach in rainy weather
Visits and romantic gestures
Kisses in the park
Rushing the work day to lay eyes on him
How did this all come from a spark?

In The Meantime

> Falling in love
> No better feeling
> Living in love
> A love so deep it keeps me reeling

LaRhonda N. Felton

## **Falling in Lies**

It's frightening for a stranger
To say I love you for no apparent reason
But for everything in life
There's a time and a season

I should've been alerted
When he came on way too strong
That there would be many things
I'd discover were wrong

Trying to force chemistry
When my intuition said no
I should've just listened and let him go

Tired of being alone
Craving love and closeness
Can't sacrifice too much
Especially not my happiness

The *I love yous* at the end of each call
Still weren't enough to make me fall

I wasn't feeling it
Couldn't explain why
Intuition was spot on
Because it all turned out to be a lie
I gave him the benefit of the doubt
I followed the so-called rules
Didn't want to lose out

I soon realized I wasn't losing
He was a bold-face liar
It was me he was fooling

In The Meantime

> I gathered my thoughts
> I wised up quick
> I'm a good woman
> Too good for this shit
>
> Once I'm done, it's a wrap
> No do overs and no turning back
>
> Like I said, there is always a season
> He and I were night and day
> I trusted him to be honest
> But all he did was lie for no apparent reason

LaRhonda N. Felton

## **Karma**

Hurt feelings
A cold heart
Fuck you think?
When you played a part

All lovey dovey
Into only me
All the while
A dog in heat

The old people say
Watch the company you keep
Who knew it would
Ever apply to me?

Me being me
Faithful and true
How stupid I must've looked
A damn fool for you

Cooking and cleaning
Auditioning for the wife role
Didn't know of the competition
Truth be told

Look before I leap
I was supposed to be smarter
Not fall so fast
You made that much harder

Catering to me
Listening to my dreams
Wanting them to become reality

In The Meantime

        Or so it seemed

      Oh, your turn will come
      Sooner than you think
      When the one you love
      Makes your heart sink

      I can only hope
      You handle it better than I
      Right now, my only wish
      Is that in hell you fry

LaRhonda N. Felton

## **She is Me**

I'm in love with her
She's juicy in all the right places
Booty thick like gumbo
She's soft to touch
But she can be rough and tough

She's been hurt
She's open to love
Fearless and bold
She can be warm and cold

She's a fearless protector
The troubles of the world often affect her
She's brutally honest, most of the time
She tells it straight, but she tries to be kind

She's been called an inspiration
One-of-a-kind
An anomaly
There won't ever be another
Because she is me

In The Meantime

LaRhonda N. Felton

## **Pass or Fail**

He said he thought of me
And he just couldn't do it
The love I have given him
He couldn't stand to lose it

One night with her
Wasn't worth the pain
He recalled all the times
I was there for him in the rain

I held him down
Sometimes, I held him up
Why would he risk losing me
Over a quick nut?

I'm giving him the side eye
What brought on this confession?
He couldn't see life without me
He thanks God daily, I'm his blessing

He claims it all began
As small laughs and flirting
Drinks after work
Then touching and smirking

I'm getting more heated by the minute
It wasn't just physical
Seems some emotions came with it

I keep my composure
And let him talk
He swears he didn't cheat
He's not considering the emotional part

In The Meantime

One thing led to another
They ended up in a hotel
He said I would never know
So, he figured what the hell

Something she said
Made him pause and his heart sink
It was a simple question she asked
"What is your girl going to think?"

He says that was the moment
He knew he had to leave
It was like the air had left the room
Suddenly he couldn't breathe
Grabbed his coat
Before she could speak
He cleared his throat
"Thank you," he said
"For making me see
My girl means the world to me
I don't want to live if she leaves"

So, here he is
Making this deep confession
I can never let on
I'm the teacher in this lesson

The young lady at his job
We go back a long time
I had to be sure
He was mine and all mine
I've done too much
Put in a lot of work
To watch it go up in smoke
'Cause he chasing skirts

LaRhonda N. Felton

So, I orchestrated the set up
To see if he would pass
Or if he would fall victim
To another piece of ass

# In The Meantime

LaRhonda N. Felton

## Assets

Your ass might attract him
Another ass will distract him
If ass is all you have to offer
There's another ass that's softer
When you use your ass to get ahead
Each and every time your ass will be misled
Your ass can't be your means to an end
Your ass is more valuable than the money you spend
Unless of course your ass is cheap
And you're selling your ass cheap as potted meat
Be smarter, use your brain and rest your ass
Because if ass is all you rely on, then your ass is sad

In The Meantime

LaRhonda N. Felton

## **Gone**

Why did they go?
Why did you stay?
Time can be a bitch
When one goes away
Some days drag
Others vanish quick
Will the pain ever cease?
Where's the kill switch?
The memories rush in
The tears stick around
Sleep disappears
And happiness can't be found
Things I looked forward to
Don't even matter
Thoughts are inconsistent
My brain is scattered
I pray every day
Just to make it through
Sadness consumes me
It's all darkness and gloom
Waiting for the rain to stop
And the sun to return
Before it all falls apart
And I crash and burn

In The Meantime

LaRhonda N. Felton

## **Blackout**

He races into the room
And kisses my lips
All the while insisting
She doesn't mean shit
I never saw this coming
Didn't think it would be me
My own man sleeping around
Hoeing in these streets

I want to kick his ass
Punch him the face
All the hurt I feel
An all too familiar space
But he made promises
Ones now he can never keep
As all my dreams shatter
It's as if my heart won't beat

I can't breathe
I feel so flushed
Everything is spinning
There is this rush
Suddenly all is quiet
Then something hits the floor
I remember nothing
Security kicks in the door
An escalated scene
They look from him to me
My focus is clearer
I see he's bleeding
He's angry but alive
Paramedics rush in since he's hurt
I look down and see blood all over my shirt

In The Meantime

The scene is wild
I guess I evened the score
My hand is so heavy
I'm clutching
The champagne bottle from the night before

LaRhonda N. Felton

## **Secrets**

As his tears begin to fall
We both realize it's over
No need wishing on a star
No searching for a four-leaf clover
This should've never started
I wasn't available for exclusivity
Sneaking around and stealing time
No hopes of longevity
My husband had to be my priority
My vows broken to the man I married
Unsure where it would end
Really unsure of whose baby I carried
All I can be sure of
Is I'm the mother
Can't be sure of the father
Could be my husband or my lover
This man would never know
Because I could never confess
How did my quiet life
Become such a mess?
Between me and God
This secret will be kept
I grabbed my purse
Kissed his cheek and left

# In The Meantime

LaRhonda N. Felton

## **Confession**

He can't ever know the secret I hide
It will break his heart and crush his pride

I never set out to cheat
It's just that the other guy listened to me
We only went out for drinks
Going back to his place, I didn't even think

Before I knew it, we were laughing and touching
Suddenly nothing is something
I love my man, but he hasn't been focused
Leaving me lonely and hopeless

I tried to explain I was hurt and in pain
He didn't seem to care or even understand
Hanging with the fellas all hours of the night
Never once checking to make sure I was alright

I played along, hell I'm hurting
We would talk about TV shows
And the playoff scores
He showed genuine interest in me
Even if the conversation was just about trivial things

He noticed my new perfume and pedicures
He had to have a wife, I just knew that for sure

When I got to his place
I knew that wasn't the case
Now I've made the mistake of being in his bed
If I confess, my relationship is dead

In The Meantime

My man knows something is wrong
For a week straight, he's been at home
I can't keep this secret, he must know
The beginning of my end, well, here goes…

LaRhonda N. Felton

## **Broken**

Pins and needles
Walking on eggshells
The torment of this life
Is like living in hell

I never know what
Will set him off
I try not to frustrate him
So, I rarely talk

My family is concerned
They know something is wrong
My friends no longer come around
My life is no longer my own

I belong to him
That's what he's forced me to believe
No one loves me like him
At least that's how it seems

I left after the first slap
Believing he was just drunk
I wasn't really hurt
It wasn't much more than a tap

That's how it all began
I should've seen the signs
Isolation from everyone
Him calling me all the time

## In The Meantime

A black eye, broken nose
Even a fractured hip
Suffered two miscarriages
I told the doctor I slipped

He knew I was lying
Tried forcing me to tell
I saw no way out
From this living hell

I slept with the devil
On a daily basis
He would go to work
Smiling in all the faces
A green-eyed monster
Cold and deadly
I prayed for death
I felt I was ready

No smiling for me
There was no reason
Every day of my life
Was the killing season

I knew he would do it
Take my life, that is
No one could save me
Not even the kids

The walls had caved in
I had nowhere to turn
Somehow, I had to get out
And he had to learn

LaRhonda N. Felton

The gun went off
And down he fell
Returning to his throne
In the pits of hell

# In The Meantime

LaRhonda N. Felton

## Acknowledgments

First, giving thanks to God for blessing me with this gift. I always thought writing was just a hobby until I said a prayer in December 2016 asking God to reveal to me what gift He wanted me to use immediately. The answer came in as an almost instantaneous response, and the words began pouring out. I will be forever grateful.
For the vessels that God saw fit to bring me here through, my mom Phyllis Felton and my dad Lindsey Felton, thank you. Mama, I say thank you for the love and support you've given me over the years. You have been there every step of the way. I love you very much. My father is no longer here to witness this dream finally become a reality. Daddy, you are loved and missed more than you could ever know. We learned a lot from each other and I wish we'd had more time. R.I.P.

My grandmother, Mildred Thomas, my very first best friend. You have always taught me to speak my mind. You are the strongest woman I know, and I hope this accomplishment makes you proud. The lessons you've instilled in me will take me a long way in this world. I love you so much and thank you. Thanks to my aunt Alice Elaine Dinkens. We've laughed and shared so many life lessons and you always thought I had a way with words. Thanks for believing in me. To my brother Lindsey Thomas Felton, thank you. I know I can be a handful, but you're always there when I need you. Special thanks to my cousins, Devon and Ashley Dinkens. We were raised more like siblings instead of first cousins. I love you both.

In The Meantime

To my nieces and nephews, I love you all very much. I want this to serve as an example that you can accomplish anything you put your mind to. Each one of you are talented in one form or another. Hone that talent, believe in yourself because I believe in each of you. Your dreams can become reality with hard work and dedication. "Stix", my kindred spirit, I love you and you can do it. I know you can. Thanks to the rest of my family. Each one of you has left a lasting impression on me in some way. To my book club ladies, Toni Cash Petty and Joye Powell, thank you. You ladies have been in our group since day one and we're on year fifteen. Thank you so much for being my beta readers and believing in me. I love you both and your support has been immeasurable. My sister-friend, Monica "Monet" Coleman, thank you. You have been there through thick and thin. Your support of me and this project is forever engrained in my heart. I love you, sis. To my best friend, Torrence "T-Man" Smith, thank you. You listen to me rant and rave and still find a way to make me laugh. I love you, BFF. Special thanks to Janice Parker and Cecile Waddell. You ladies came through with full support when the raffle idea didn't succeed as planned. Your contribution helped me to succeed in getting this project completed. Thank you so very much.

Many special thanks to Shanieka Moore and Gloria Barnett. You ladies read some of my work and provided feedback. I thank you both very much.

To Liltera R. Williams, I thank you so very much for helping me make this dream a reality. You have been a God send. I look forward to many more projects in the future. To all others, I hope that you find joy and laughter in reading my finished project. I thank you so very much.

LaRhonda N. Felton

## About the Author

Although Author LaRhonda N. Felton's love for writing was recognized and nurtured early, she often struggled with taming the habit of censorship. Even after winning second place in a short story contest in $8^{th}$ grade and later having one of her poems published in a national anthology, it took more time to fully acknowledge her undying passion for the craft.

With a myriad of life experiences to draw from, LaRhonda's forward-thinking ideas on love and life soon began to pour out at an uncontrollable rate. A self-proclaimed realist who is admired by most for her honesty, she learned how to simply let the words flow, no longer concerned about who the truth may offend. This unrestricted freedom of expression allowed her to discover a personal niche, strictly focusing on the erotic aspects of adulthood.

*In The Meantime* is her first published collection of poetry, but she already has three completed manuscripts on standby.

# In The Meantime

124

www.ingramcontent.com/pod-product-compliance
Lightning Source LLC
Chambersburg PA
CBHW020427010526
44118CB00010B/455